Hamsters
& Gerbils

K.W. Smith

G000093827

John Bartholomew & Son Limited
Edinburgh

First published in Great Britain 1976 by
JOHN BARTHOLOMEW & SON LIMITED
12 Duncan Street, Edinburgh EH9 1TA

ISBN 0 7028 1082 7

1st edition
Reprinted 1982, 1984

Designed and illustrated by Allard Design Group Limited
Printed in Great Britain by John Bartholomew & Son Limited

Acknowledgements
Thanks are due to the following for their assistance in the production of this book:
The National Mongolian Gerbil and Small Rodents Society, and the British
Federation of Hamster Clubs for kind permission to use their show standards.

Contents

Introduction

One of the most common small pets in Britain, America, and around the world was known to science only as a skeleton, less than fifty years ago. That skeleton has since sprouted flesh, and the Golden Hamster, in all its colour variations, is so popular that a club has been formed to foster interest in keeping the animal not only as a pet but for exhibition purposes.

The story of the Golden Hamster began in the late 1830s when a skeleton was found and classified as a member of the family *cricetidae* in the sub-order *myomorpha* (mouse-like rodents) in the order *rodentia*. Almost a century later, in 1930, the first living specimen of *Mesocricetus auratus,* the Golden or Syrian Hamster, was discovered near Aleppo : an adult female with twelve young.

In the following year two pairs of hamsters were sent to Britain for use in laboratories, from where further specimens were duly sent to the United States, again for laboratory research : the public were almost unaware of the existence of these beautiful rodents.

Not until the end of the Second World War was the Golden Hamster released as a pet, when it proceeded to capture the hearts of animal lovers everywhere with its friendly nature and cleanliness, traits that have now placed it among the front ranks for popularity.

The Common Hamster, *Cricetus cricetus,* is much more plentiful, and lives in the wooded steppes of Eastern Europe, where it is forced to hibernate each winter.

Side by side with the hamsters in the evolutionary chain, come the gerbils, *gerbillinae*, which, although known to science for a much longer time, have made an even greater and more recent impact as pets. While the hamsters went westbound over the Atlantic, the gerbils came east ; the Mongolian Gerbil was introduced to the United States in the early 1950s for use in research – prompted by its high resistance to radiation – and was found to be equally successful as a pet when it was launched on the market in 1964. The gerbil was introduced to the British public soon after, and made such an impact that a club was formed to further the cause of the animal not only in Britain but around the world.

Gerbils and rats, and deer mice, are close relations within the family *cricetidae,* cousins to the dormice and the *muridae,* the rats and the mice proper, and more distantly related to the kangaroo rats. They are all rodents, an order which is divided into three groups according to the position and structure of the jaw muscles, and which includes such exotic animals as the gopher, the chipmunk, the jerboa, the capybara, the porcupine, and that old favourite, the guinea-pig.

In the wild, gerbils (pronounced with a soft G, as the G in Germany) range over the sandy plains and steppes of Mongolia and China, the Thar Desert of India and Pakistan, and in the northern Sahara, but we shall be considering only *Meriones unguichlatus,* the Mongolian member of the tribe, an animal four inches long with a tail as long again.

Choosing a pet

With no criticism of pet stores intended, I would suggest the person who is buying a hamster or gerbil for the first time, or who intends to breed for exhibition, should visit a stud farm where only the best-quality exhibition stock is kept. Subsequent purchases, or animals bought merely for a companion, may be bought at the pet store, which caters more particularly for the general market.

There are a number of points to watch for in the actual selection, some obvious and others more obscure. Gerbils should be full of life and very inquisitive, with wide-open eyes and a good sheen on the coat ; any sign of drowsiness should be taken as an indication of poor condition or possibly illness.

Less obviously, the animal should have certain other qualities : there should be no bald spots, scabs or sores, missing or damaged claws, kinks or swellings on the tail — which, ending in a tifted tip, is essential to the animal's balance while standing erect. The intending purchaser would do well to study the show standards and apply some if not all of these to the animal he considers buying.

The same general conditions apply to the selection of a hamster, except that since it is in nature nocturnal, some degree of daytime drowsiness may be acceptable.

Additionally, the hamster's coat needs to be examined : a young animal will have paler and patchier colouring, so one must be able to distinguish between a healthy immature hamster and an undersized runt adult which may be no larger but which will have a richer and more uniform coat. The experienced hamster-breeder will at once be able to distinguish adult from juvenile, since the latter will have a mass of fine, silky, light-grey hair in the ear orifice, which disappears as the animal matures.

The coat must also be examined just under the tail. While any stains could be merely a passing attack of diarrhoea caused by too moist a diet, the same symptoms could indicate an attack of wet

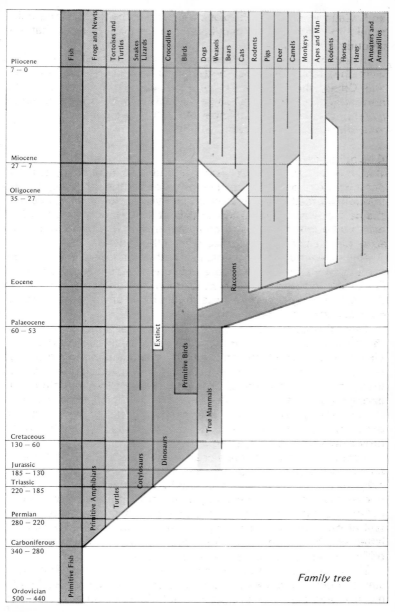

Family tree

tail, an ailment fatal to hamsters. Naturally any animal stained around the anal fur should not be bought, and as a precaution against spreading the highly contagious disease, the hands should be washed as soon as possible.

Six weeks is the most suitable age at which to buy a hamster. At this age it may still be somewhat nervous and may even bite, but it will very quickly accept the change of surroundings and learn to trust its new owner.

Those new surroundings will come quicker than expected if one goes to buy a hamster without taking an adequate carrying cage or well-ventilated biscuit tin. I have often seen hamsters put into cardboard boxes for the journey home, the owners forgetting that this rodent in particular can chew through cardboard almost as fast as it can eat a lettuce leaf.

A good sturdy carrying cage with a glass front, adequate food and bedding material, and a private corner, is the best way of ensuring that the hamster reaches home – where a proper, permanent cage should already have been prepared to receive it.

Housing

All too many cages offered on the retail market are designed to catch the eye of the pet owner, and tend to put the animals' needs last, economizing just a little too much on that vital ingredient for happiness – space.

A hamster should have a minimum of 200 square inches of floor space – a cage 20in x 10in – and at least 8in headroom; the floor area should be increased by at least half for a cage holding two females, while a more specialist design is recommended for a breeding pair. Two gerbils will be happy in the 200 square inch cage, but since these animals enjoy jumping they should not be denied any extra inches of headroom that can be provided.

The breeder who wishes to build his own cages can use half-inch planed floorboarding, equally stout chipboard, or, if money is no problem, very thick plywood; the basic essential is that the cage be as gnawproof as possible and be made of a non-toxic material for those occasions when a hamster will get the urge to try out its teeth on the inner walls. Although timber is referred to as a construction material, the handyman able to work in metals may find his skills readily adaptable to the challenge. The use of moulded fibreglass, or any form of plastic lining, should be ruled out as these materials constitute a serious risk of poisoning.

The furnishings of the cage are simple: a good layer of clean sawdust or dried peat mixed with sand should cover the floor, and while hamsters will appreciate a separate nest box, gerbils will be able to make use of a well-dried-out section from a tree branch, with a sizeable hole drilled in it for use as a nest.

The hamster nest box should not rob the cage floor of any useable space. It can be fixed to the side, with a ladder for access, or it can be put on an intermediate shelf, again with a simple ladder or branch for the animal to climb. The box itself, made of timber, must be no smaller than 6 inches square with two entrance holes in the side and a lift-off lid, which makes periodic cleaning of the box and observation of the animals easy.

Gerbils do not appreciate this conventional type of box, preferring to build their own nest in one corner, and then demolishing it a short while later to rebuild it elsewhere, either in the hollowed trunk provided or in some other niche that offers some temporary allure.

Both the hamster nest box, and the gerbil cage, must have adequate nesting material constantly available. Clean, dry hay and a few dried autumn leaves are acceptable, but the pet owner should make certain that no diseased matter is introduced, since in the confines of a cage there is no opportunity for the animals to discard unwanted vegetation, nor to vacate a nest site that has fungus or parasites.

This everyday cage, like the other specialized cages – for carrying animals to a show, for displaying them once there, and for nursing them through illness – must be kept scrupulously clean at all times, the hamster cage being thoroughly scoured out once a week, the gerbil home once a fortnight, with all nest material and floor covering replaced. These routine scourings should be done with hot water and disinfectant, allowing the cage to dry thoroughly before the occupants are returned to it. When breeding hamsters and gerbils one can never really have too many cages.

Every few weeks the disinfecting should be a little more rigorous, playing the flame from a blowlamp all over the cage interior, except, of course, the glass front panel. The most likely troublespots in any cage are the corners, and it is in here that triangular wedges should be fitted, of the type sold to prevent dust collecting in the angles on stair treads.

The positioning of the cages is as important as their maintenance. Although gerbils are creatures of the hot desert regions, they are not lovers of the heat; their cages should not only be out of the direct sunlight, but also in a spot where fresh air can readily circulate. Since the animals are small, they can readily lose too much body heat, even through their fur, so the provision of fresh air must not entail cold draughts. Remembering, too, that hamsters hibernate in the wild, they will need to follow their natural rhythms in captivity if they are in a position to sympathize with and respond to the rhythm of the seasons: the owner who wants to appreciate his *mesocricetus* all winter long will have to ensure the animal is in regular artificial light and an equable temperature.

While the cage is in effect a prison, the animal must think of it rather as a home – and to this end it must have a selection of toys and furnishings. Rodents are sufficiently high up the evolutionary ladder not only to appreciate playthings, but also to invent games suitable for them. The yardstick should, of course, not be whether the toy 'looks nice', but whether it simulates conditions in the wild. Thus an empty jam jar or earthenware pot – the kind honey was sold in years ago – appear, to the animals, as small burrows in the ground.

Hamsters will use these as food stores (the owner must remove

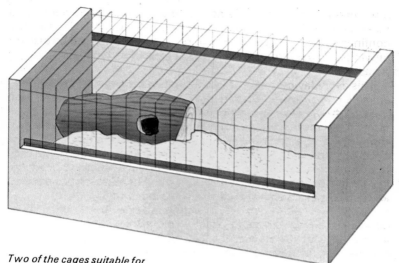

Two of the cages suitable for hamsters or gerbils

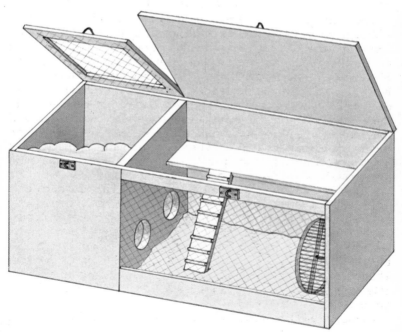

any food that goes mouldy) in preparation for the normally lean months of winter – or, conveniently, as lavatories. Gerbils, who burrow to escape the desert heat by day and cold by night, will spend many happy hours inside their artificial tunnels.

Other playthings can consist of small branches, wooden cotton reels, or, for hamsters, metal exercise wheels that either do not have the axle continuing through the centre or are sufficiently large for it not to rub on the animal's back, causing sores. Gerbils should not have these wheels since for them there is the much greater risk of catching the tail between the treads, either skinning or breaking the delicate balancing organ. With this exception, the range of potential toys is as long as the owner's imagination, bearing in mind the essential safety factors: nothing made from plastics or rubbers; nothing painted; and nothing with sharp points or edges.

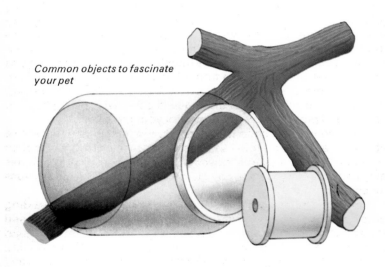

Common objects to fascinate your pet

Handling and taming

Among the many predators of wild rodents are foxes and birds of prey, either of which will seize its victim roughly by the middle. Therefore, the breeder who inadvertently attempts to pick up his pet in the same manner will merely release the pent-up terror passed on by generations of in-bred instinct: the animal will retaliate in the only way it can, and the disillusioned owner will almost certainly have a bitten finger.

Handling must be done slowly and in full view of the animal, especially in the early days of the pet/owner relationship. One of the easiest ways is to scoop the creature up in both hands, closing thumb and forefinger to prevent escape and the risk of injury.

One can pick a gerbil up by the base of the tail – anywhere else can result in the tail being skinned or broken – immediately transferring it to the upturned palm of the free hand, but still retaining a grip on the tail. Or one can pick up either animal from above, giving notice of intent from the outset. Approaching the animal from the front, stroke the back, pausing just past the high point as the spine begins to dip towards the tail. The thumb can now move in gently to the belly area immediately in front of the hind leg, while the tips of the fingers move in from the animal's other side. Lift gently, transfer the pet to the other palm: the move is done with no frightening actions and provides no opportunity for your pet to bite.

Since young and timid hamsters often create a minor defensive attack in any case – one sharp nip is usually the limit of their assault – the hand can be gloved in the earlier days, although this may partly defeat the object by giving the animal a little more cause for anxiety.

Handling the animals is the first step in the slow but rewarding process of taming them, and should be allied with affection and reward. The pets can be induced to approach the outstretched hand by holding a peanut or piece of cheese between the fintertips, and once they have been picked up and transferred to the other open hand, a little stroking and carressing, again with a titbit, will soon create pleasant associations with what is basically an indignity – bodily moving the animal from the place of *its* choice to the place of its owner's choice.

Gerbils, being inquisitive little creatures, are more easily handled than are the shyer hamsters, but neither can inflict a harmful bite on a human.

The human voice is of far greater importance in the taming of

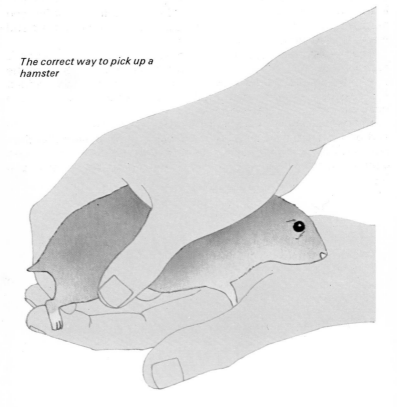

The correct way to pick up a hamster

14

animals than might at first appear; while the words of course mean nothing at all — neither hamsters nor gerbils will ever respond to an individual name — the intonation and the volume say a great deal. During the process of introducing the hand to the animal, and while lifting and stroking, the owner should continue talking softly and reassuringly, thus building one more link in the chain of trust and respect, out of which will come affection.

The animal in its cage will in time become aware of its owner's approach by the familiar sounds — whatever they may be — of the shed door opening and the food bin rattling: when to this is added the reassurance of the voice and the recognizable human smell, the pet is a long way on the road to tameness.

Cat owners know their animals love to be stroked under the chin and on the cheek; so gerbil owners will very soon learn that their pets respond well to being fussed and having their head and ears gently tickled. A little goes a long way, and soon the gerbil is a friend for life.

Offer a timid gerbil a tit-bit

Sexing, breeding and rearing

Breeding hamsters and gerbils is no easy operation; introducing the male of the species *mesocricetus* to the female is a delicate task that must be timed exactly, and incautious attempts at getting the *gerbillinae* to procreate can so easily end with the male being killed.

Hamsters

In the normal course of events, hamsters should never be expected to share the territory of their cage – the only exceptions being during mating and the subsequent rearing of the young by the female. Regardless of whether like sexes or opposite sexes are housed together, fighting will always result, leading in time to the inevitable death of one party. Thus, if the animals are to make love, not war, a complicated ritual must be followed.

The easiest way is to prepare a special honeymoon cage (the size ratio was discussed in the chapter on housing) which is essentially a split compartment, a fine wire mesh on a timber frame being slid down the centre.

A week or so before it is estimated that the female will come on heat, the male is introduced to the entire cage, the divider not being in place: this now becomes the male's territory, impregnated with his own particular scent. Since some miscalculations are bound to occur as to when the female actually comes into season, the male may spend well over a week in this new, larger home.

The female's oestrus cycle recurring about every fourth day, the owner should have some good idea of when he wishes the mating to occur. He must, however, examine the female carefully for signs of the cycle's peak – an increase in her activity combined with a slight swelling and reddening of the vaginal opening: this is the ideal time for mating and the deadline for which he must aim.

Difficulties arise because the exact time is learned only by experience – with a cycle so short, the peak fertility time is also so much more acute – and the breeder must anticipate this time pretty accurately.

Some hours – or a day – before this climax is due, the male must be removed from his cage to some other prepared home that does not bear the scent of his mate-to-be. She is then taken from her cage and put in the honeymoon compartment alone. She must be allowed to run around the place so that she can accept it as her own home, one in which she is not the interloper; in doing so, she will of course lay her own scent over that of the recently removed male.

Some two or three hours later the female, nearing her climax, is confined to one half of the cage by the lowering of the central divider. The male is now reintroduced to the other side of the divider. He is back in his home environment, but is at once aware from the odour that a female of the species has passed that way.

Presently the two animals will come face to face, only the wire mesh separating them; they will sniff at each other, and the female will make the decision. If she snaps, attempting to attack the male, then mating on this particular occasion will not take place and she may be returned to her own cage.

If she freezes rigid, and if her tail rises slightly when her back is stroked, she has accepted her partner and is ready to mate — although, once the dividing mesh has been removed and the male allowed to mount the female, she may yet change her mind and announce it with a sudden attack on her partner. The pair should be left together for no longer than it takes to perform the act, and they should not go unobserved.

His duty done, the male can then be transferred to the cage originally inhabited by the female, she being allowed to occupy the honeymoon compartment until the family is born.

The hamster gestation period is from 15 to 17 days, the first visible signs of pregnancy coming on the seventh or eighth day, after which the animal should be handled as little as possible, and picked up only by the double-scoop method to avoid injury to the unborn.

From this time the in-cub female should receive extra protein and vitamin in the diet, which should also have its fat and carbo-hydrate content slightly reduced to avoid obesity other than by the pregnancy itself. Powdered non-fat milk may also supplement the drinking water.

On the twelfth day the bedding and floor-covering should be replaced, allowing the animal to build its nest with the best possible materials in preparation for the birth, which will usually take place in late evening or early morning, the times of greatest activity in the animal's body-clock.

The litter will vary from one to around sixteen, but usually averaging seven blind, deaf, toothless, and bald blobs of pink flesh with bulging black blobs where the eyes will soon appear at four days the skin begins to darken, at six the fur appears, at eight the ears open, and between ten and twelve days of age the eyelids roll back.

METHOD OF MATING HAMSTERS

Now the honeymoon cage will be home to a pack of adventurous cubs who wander freely into every corner, rapidly gaining strength, size, and the full features of the adolescent hamster, until somewhere between the age of twenty and thirty days the mother will begin to tire of their playfulness and of her responsibility, and begin bullying.

It is the sign that family life is over, and the now tired female should be removed from her honeymoon home and returned to a normal-sized cage to lead her usual unruffled existence.

Between the ages of four and five weeks the young themselves must go their separate ways as they are fast approaching sexual maturity and would inevitably attempt to breed — and fight — if left together. By ten weeks each animal must have its own individual cage, and not be introduced to another of its own species until the honeymoon compartment is again called into use.

Gerbils

Family life among the gerbils is entirely different. They are not lovers of solitude, preferring to be in twos — a sexed pair for mating, or two females together — or in colonies: indeed, many people go as far as saying that gerbils mate for life, although the truth of this is in some doubt.

Even so, mating still has its difficulties. A sexed pair cannot be left together indefinitely, or their offspring will soon be out of all proportion to the average breeder's housing capacity, resulting in numerous quarrels among the animals and the death of some of them.

Therefore, the male has to be introduced to the female for the purposes of procreation only. In view of the monogamous habit of the animals, it is surely preferable to follow the code of nature and have just two gerbils in the mating cage. But, since there are distinct advantages in trio breeding (one male and two females) of fancy mice — this is discussed in the companion volume — a number of gerbil breeders have adopted the trio policy, not with complete success, since there are reported instances of the females ganging up on the lone male so much that he has been afraid to come out of hiding and feed.

Let us have just one female for the male's desires, and let us put each animal in one half of the divided honeymoon cage, as used with the hamsters. This time there is no need for the elaborate process of establishing supremacy; each animal can go into a clean compartment and get accustomed to it as well as to the presence of

METHODS OF MATING GERBILS

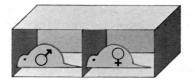

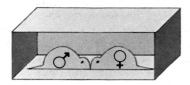

a) Introduce male and female to divided cage. After 2–3 days allow mating.

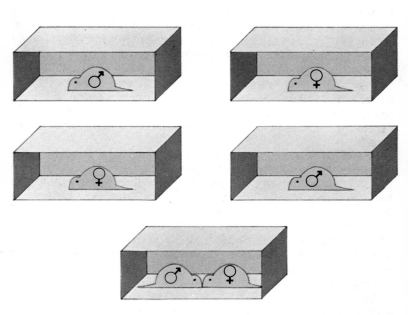

b) Put male and female into their own fresh cages. Swap cages so they acquire other's scent. Introduce them to the breeding cage.

its neighbour through the wire mesh. Two or three days later, the divider removed, the animals confront each other as equals: they will either accept each other and settle down quite quickly as a pair, or — much less likely — will fight. In this instance the best course is to start again with two other gerbils in fresh bedding in the same box — unless, of course, due to the demands of a breeding programme, one of the earlier-selected animals is needed for stock, when it would be better to try with a fresh mate and a fresh cage.

There is another way of making the introduction: put a male and female each in its own clean, fresh cage for a day, then swap them into the other's cage for another day, so that each acquires the other's scent. On the third day put them both, at the same time, into the breeding cage. Allow a little while for the pair to settle down, then leave them to mate, which will usually occur within the week and usually in the evening: during this premarital period the animals should be handled only when absolutely necessary.

The gestation period for gerbils is 23 to 25 days, a little longer than for hamsters, and the father-to-be may remain in the cage throughout the confinement, delivery, and weaning; indeed, he will share in the upbringing of his young in a way that no male hamster would.

The gerbil cubs at birth are a little under an inch long, pink, blind, deaf, and toothless; the average litter has five cubs, but the number can be much more.

At four days old the skin turns dark, growing a fine coat of seal-grey fur at six days, by which time the ears have opened. The young can see at two weeks of age, when they begin practising gnawing with their newly emerged teeth. A week after that — with the mother exhausting herself with the care she devotes to the young — the cubs will begin eating solid food and weaning can begin. Between five and six weeks after birth the parents should be removed from the cage, allowing the young to achieve their independence.

And now comes another problem.

While the female can join another of her sex in a cage of their own, this is hardly practicable for the male, since the two will have to fight to establish supremacy. If the male and female are left together, then of course a second litter will be the result. If the male is simply introduced to, or perhaps even returned to, a colony of gerbils, his group scent will have been lost and he will be the victim of attack by the other males, frequently resulting in his death.

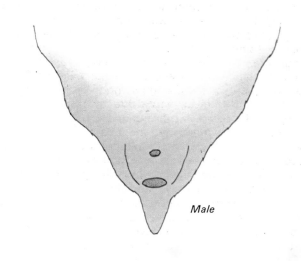

Male

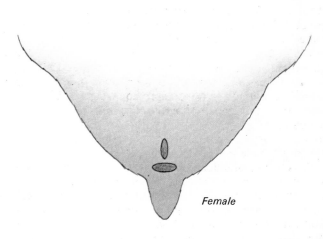

Female

SEXING GERBILS

If he is not to lead a life of isolation as a reward for his breeding tactics, he must first reacquire the group scent by having his fur slightly rubbed with urine-dampened bedding from the colonial cage. He can then be returned, but the prudent owner will keep a careful check for an hour or so to see that acceptance is achieved.

A colony of gerbils, usually housed in a very large cage, perhaps occupying an entire bench in a shed, is usually the progeny of a breeding couple or their litter. As will be seen later, colonial life is no answer for the breeder who is pursuing a special bloodline – nor is it a wise way of keeping gerbils unless the owner can reach an understanding with a pet shop about taking his surplus stock.

Although gerbils are prolific breeders, they do not have the population potential of some of the other rodents. A female gerbil, mated at ten to twelve weeks, can have ten to twelve litters in her period of fertility, which declines rapidly at the age of fourteen to sixteen months – although pregnancies much later than this are not unknown, even though the litters are inferior in number and virility. A fair maximum for any gerbil would be eight pregnancies, after which the animal should be left with members of her own sex at least until she has permanently ceased to ovulate.

Neither hamsters nor gerbils should be allowed to breed before ten weeks of age since this can stunt the female's growth, shorten her life, and result in inferior young.

Sexing

The easiest time to distinguish the sex of both families of rodent is between the ages of three and four weeks when the fur has not completely covered the developing sex organs.

Holding a hamster by the scruff of the neck – an action which should be reserved for this purpose alone, since it offends the animal's dignity – one can observe that in the female the genital and the anal openings are quite close, whereas in the male the scrotum is further removed from the anus, and is a little more prominent. The female's body tapers towards the rear more than does the male's.

In the gerbil, however, the reverse is true: the male's body tapers more. Sexing in gerbils, apart from this peculiarity, is exactly the same as in hamsters, with the additional help of a large dark patch (pink in albinos) on the lower underside of the male.

Runts and Mutations

A runt is a weak and often undersized animal born in a litter. While some species ruthlessly kill oif their runts, almost as if they had read Darwin's theory on the survival of the fittest, a mother gerbil will frequently give her own runt offspring more attention than average, even going to the point of building it a separate nest.

Most runts never reach maturity, although they enjoy to the full the limited life that is granted to them. But the runt should never be used for breeding.

The colour mutation is equally as unpredictable as the runt, but is always something that is desirable from the breeding point of view. The amateur rodent keeper who suspects he has a mutant should contact a reputable breeder or the appropriate society for advice on how to perpetuate the new strain which, if lost in this generation, may be gone for ever.

Breeding Methods

In addition to the problems incurred in getting the animals to breed, the person who is striving for a particular end product has the task of breeding selectively. Without delving too far into the science of genetics, three basic methods can be quoted:

In-breeding. Let us assume we are trying to improve the spot which is evident on the heads of two related gerbils of opposite sex. If we breed from these the chances are good that in at least two cubs – one of each sex – the spot will be a little nearer the desired result. The feature is now to be bred into the strain, by mating these two from the same litter, and selecting the best from their offspring. By careful selection within each generation, the ultimate result will be an animal with exactly the marking required – but the selection must truly be very carefully done, or undesirable characteristics will also be fixed in the strain, some of which (like a tendency to cannibalism) may not be evident until too late. It is this side-effect which has cast something of a slur on this method of breeding.

Breeding back. Assuming we are again faced with the problem of how to improve a gerbil's spot in succeeding generations, but this time with only one such animal from which to breed, we must of necessity introduce a mate without the required marking. In the cubs resulting from this mating, the quality of the spot will vary from very good to very bad.

The offspring which shows the spot to the best effect is now selected and mated with its spotted parent – and is later mated with its own selected offspring from that union, a method which will, in time, all but eliminate the blood line of the original un-

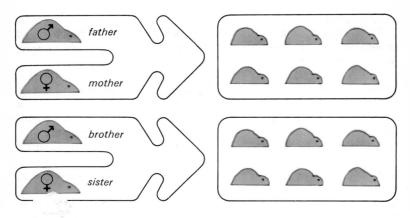

▲ *IN-BREEDING. Mate pair with inferior markings. From this litter mate superior brother and sister.*

▼ *BREEDING BACK. Mate one marked with an unmarked. From their litter mate the best marked cub with the parent.*

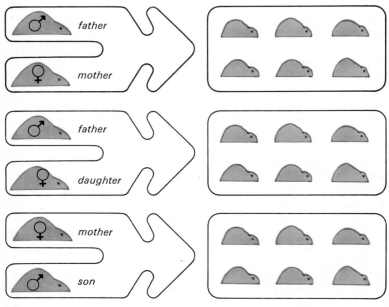

spotted cross.

The basic methods now become apparent in that the first method is selective within the same generation while the second bridges back a generation.

Line Breeding. A more detailed study of genetics will reveal what has already been hinted at — that in-breeding can result in a weakening of other traits while strengthening the one that has been selected. Line breeding goes some way to solving the problem.

It is obviously helpful to have two distinct strains of in-bred animals running concurrently: not only are one's chances of success doubled, but one's risks of failure are halved. However, at about the fifth generation of the line, an out-cross can be made: a male mating not with his sister but with his cousin three times removed. This can be the beginning of another line to be in-bred, while still retaining the other two; it could also be the signal to phase out one of the strains, although by doing this one loses the later opportunity of injecting another genetic shot-in-the-arm.

A selected cub from the out-cross litter could also be bred back again or in-bred: the combinations begin to multiply.

The key to successful selective breeding does not lie in choosing from the entire stock the buck and doe which come closest to the desired effect, then throwing their young back into the melting-pot and starting again on the same principle: this is chancing to luck. One must create continuity of the blood lines at all costs, whether it is strengthened by the occasional out-cross or refined by continual in-breeding.

At this point the need for good, detailed, accurate labelling systems and record cards becomes apparent — so also does the need for an outlet for the animals that are not selected for breeding!

Fostering

Sometime, somewhere down the blood line, every breeder will come upon a mother who cannot or will not rear her young. There are several causes: the mother may be too young or the litter too big; she may succumb to a chill; she may not be able to lactate sufficiently; or she may not want the bother.

There is only one way of saving the threatened young — by fostering them onto another mother with a small litter of about the same age.

An obvious precaution for a breeder who is reaching a critical time in the development of a strain of gerbils, is to have another female mated at the same time as the prize specimen; this is perhaps the basis for the adoption of the trio mating system — one male being allowed to impregnate two females in the same nest at the same time. The dangers have already been discussed but there are some advantages.

The gerbil breeder who has not adopted the trio method — and the hamster breeder (for trio mating is totally out of the question here) — will need to introduce the abandoned litter to its foster mother with minimum fuss and delay.

If the youngsters are strange to the foster parent, she will not accept them. If, however, she is removed from her nest and young, and the introduced youngsters are gently dabbed with her own urine-moistened bedding material and then mixed with her natural offspring, she is almost certain to accept them without trouble. In the rare instance of her suspicion being aroused, she must be removed again and the whole process repeated. If she refuses a second time, then either a second foster mother must be found or the young given up for lost. Refusal is, luckily, rare — the author has never lost any young gerbils due to refusal, and only two hamster cubs.

Record Cards

Records, so important to the serious breeder, must supply all the clues to identity and ancestry of each animal which is likely to be called upon for a contribution to the genetic chain — runts and others not selected (for example, the members of a strain which develops the refusal or inability to care for its young) also need records, although less elaborate.

The card itself should be fixed to the outside of the animal's cage, and should bear all the relevant information from this list:

Identification: *males are usually given a code letter, females a code number.*

Pedigree: i.e. *twelfth generation of the strain, plus parents' code letters and figures.*

Number born in litter:

Date of birth:

Dates of subsequent matings of this animal:

Code identification of sex partner:

Number born to it in each litter: *for females only.*

BREEDING REGISTER
(PEDIGREE)

SEX_____ DATE OF BIRTH_____

COLOUR AND MARKINGS_____

TYPE_____ FUR_____

SIZE_____ TAIL (GERBILS)_____

TUFT (GERBILS)_____ NAILS (GERBILS)_____

EYES_____ EARS_____

CONDITION_____

SIRE_____ DAME_____

G.SIRE_____ G.DAME_____

G.SIRE_____ G.DAME_____

REMARKS_____

_____

_____

A loose-leaf record book — the stud book — should also be kept, duplicating all this information as well as giving the detailed ancestral chain of the main animals in any breeding strain; the really serious breeder will soon find himself with a complicated family tree starting with Ax1 and ending, perhaps, ten generations later with the problem of whether to inbreed 43 with ZF or cross-breed with AL. The stud book and the pedigree will hint of many of the advantages and disadvantages from such a move, and the owner will be able to predict with accuracy the outcome of either mating.

The breeder who is perfecting a strain may also find it prudent to have a code within his code — for example, the first generation male is called AA; the males from the litter produced by his mating with the desired female shall be called ABA, ABB, ABC, and ABD, while the third generation males will be ACA, ACB, ACC, ACD, etc. Thus, at a glance, the breeder will know that his desired strain always carries the prefix A in the male; the second letter identifying how far the strain has progressed in generations, and the third letter identifying the individual in each generation.

If AA is called on to sire a second litter the males from this cross (even if the mother is the same) could be called BBA, BBB, BBC, etc, and the males from the selected sire in this generation would then be BCA, BCB, BCD, etc.

The females can be similarly figure coded, using full points where the numbers exceed ten. Thus, the third female to be named in the twelfth generation of the original cross between A and 1, would be 1.12.3. Adopted in this manner there is no likelihood of the animal's identify being confused with her date of birth, since it would be a miracle indeed to have 75 or more females born in one litter.

Feeding

The best way to understand any animal's feeding habits and needs is to examine its behaviour in the wild. The gerbil lives in semi-desert conditions and survives on a diet which is almost totally one of dried foodstuff, including ripe seeds : the few green leaves it may eat will be specially adapted to retain moisture. The animal's digestive system is able to produce sufficient water in the break-down of the cell structure of the food : in the wild it never drinks. Its urine is highly concentrated and its faeces have every vestige of liquid reabsorbed by the large intestine.

Food is available at all times of the year, and the animal has no need to hibernate nor to make provision for lean times.

The wild Common Hamster, *cricetus cricetus,* found in the wood-lands of Eastern Europe, gains its moisture from the mass of vegetation it eats, some of which is stored in its mouth pouches and later transferred to caches near its nest. Because of the fluctuating seasons it needs a food reserve, but it will hibernate during the worst of the winter.

In captivity these same traits show themselves in the hamster's habit of secreting food in any convenient corner. This habit cannot be broken − it would be wrong to try − but the owner must be careful to remove all moist food from these caches before it goes mouldy.

The amount of food to give one's animals depends largely on the individual appetite, but a rough guide is one tablespoonful of dried food per day for either hamsters or gerbils, the former having its diet supplemented with enough green food to keep it happy.

A basic diet is hamster mix, which can usually be bought from pet stores, but the discerning breeder who is cautious of cheap imitation could very well make his own bulk diet from a fair mixture of assorted grain, peanuts in their shells (the shells are beneficial, and this way there is no risk that the nuts are salted), flaked and whole maize, broken dog or cat biscuits, rabbit pellets, and assorted bird seeds. The animals − gerbils in particular − are very fond of sun-flower seeds, but while these represent an extremely useful source of vitamins and protein, they should not be given *ad lib,* or the pets will put on too much weight.

While this, plus a variety of green food (listed later), comprises a perfectly satisfactory diet, animals − like humans − appreciate a variation in the basic meal.

A mash mixture is one luxury, and this can be made with soaked

VITAMINS ESSENTIAL TO A HEALTHY DIET

Vitamin A	Cod-liver oil, milk, eggs, carrots. Essential in building disease immunity. Helps eyes to perceive light.
Vitamin B	Bran, yeast, liver. Essential to nervous system/digestion.
Vitamin C	Fruits, green vegetables, potatoes. Essential for good skin/fur condition.
Vitamin D	Cod-liver oil, milk, cheese, eggs. Helps to convert calcium and phosphorous to make bones/teeth.
Vitamin E	Helps to reduce risk of sterility.

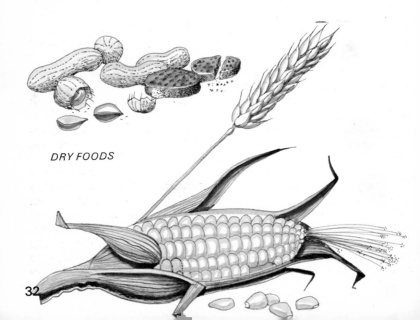

DRY FOODS

dog biscuits, crushed and bound with sufficient milk or beef stock to make a firm cake-mix consistency. To this can also be added wheat germ, canary seed, corn flakes prepared for human consumption, or milled oats; an alternative mixture of milled oats and chopped vegetable matter is often appreciated. Troubles will arise only if the mix is consistently too wet, when the animals' digestive systems will be overtaxed in extracting the moisture.

Tit-bits, offered as rewards, are also a useful source of nourishment. Both species seem to favour almost anything that is not soggy or mouldy, and favour a menu of such items as:

hard-baked bread	cheese
hard-boiled eggs	unsalted potato crisps
dog biscuits	dampened fish food
meal worms	fishing maggots (gentles)

Uneaten meal worms or maggots must be removed at once, since they will otherwise eat the remaining food and eventually pupate, to emerge as flies.

A really special treat is afforded in the form of 'nibble bars'. The recipe calls for 4oz of cornflour, an equal amount of dry wheat germ, and 8 oz of mixed corn, or hamster mix, or a combination of both, with water or milk to bind.

The cornflour and wheat germ are mixed with a little water or milk, and the whole mixture kneaded to make a stiff dough. This should be rolled on greaseproof paper, cut into strips and baked until hard in a low oven. The biscuits will keep indefinitely if stored in an airtight container.

There is a controversy over the question of whether to supply drinking water, particularly to gerbils. The author's view is that since a drink has always been appreciated by the animals, it should at least be available.

Milk is also appreciated, and supplies some of the necessary vitamins, but to avoid the offensive smell of sour milk it is preferable to give this in the form of reconstituted powder.

Whichever liquid is given to the pet it must be available in a manner which prevents it being contaminated, or being upset in the cage and so becoming a contaminant itself. Both gravity-feed water bottles and heavy open pots have advantages and drawbacks. Gravity bottles are perhaps the better option, despite the greater difficulty in fixing them, since they prevent airborne contamination of the water or milk; they are, though, prone to spontaneous leaking if a piece of the nesting material is allowed to come into contact

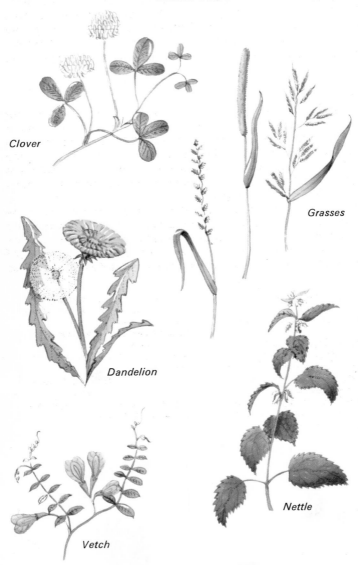

Clover

Grasses

Dandelion

Nettle

Vetch

with the spout. Open pots, although extremely difficult to overturn, do allow the risk of impurities entering the water, and they therefore need to be cleaned frequently. Further caution with the gravity bottle is needed since the spout end should be of non-corrosive metal, plastic being too easy to gnaw, and glass presenting its own hazards.

Green food

Almost any cultivated green food can be given in safety, but cabbage tends to make the urine smelly, and carrots will stain the fur if allowed to come in contact with it. While the hamster would live perfectly happily on nothing but vegetation of this nature, the desert-frequenting gerbil should have only tiny amounts not more frequently than twice a week. In either instance uneaten food must be removed the next morning.

Wild vegetation must be selected with care : not only can some plants kill by the poisons they synthesize — rhubarb leaves are a good example — but they can also be lethal from the insecticides that may be present on them. The safe list of wild plants — many of which also have applications as herbal cures, as detailed later — is thus :

Chickweed, *for an easily digestible tonic;*
Clover, *beneficial to the nervous system;*
Coltsfoot, *which eases the suffering with colds;*
Comfrey, *renowned for centuries for its helath-giving properties;*
Cow *or* **Hedge Parsley;**
Dandelion *leaves for general blood conditioning, although these can cause extra urination;*

Dead Nettle, *for its minerals;*
Dock *leaves, antiseptic internally as well as externally;*
Fresh Grasses *for their minerals and vitamins;*
Groundsel, *also a rich source of minerals;*
Plantain *and* **Shepherd's Purse,** *for their astringent qualities;*
Sorrel, Vetch, *and* **Yarrow,** *for general conditioning.*

Ailments and their treatment

From wild plants as food to wild plants as herbal cures is but a short and logical step. Many of the plants which hamsters and gerbils can be given as supplements to their basic diet are also known to have medicinal qualities – the rodent breeder who lives on the latitude of the North European Plain and in similar climates elsewhere should recognize many of the plants as weeds in the average garden.

Medicinally, plants have three applications : an infusion from the leaves may be administered as a liquid tonic ; the part-infused leaves may themselves be applied as a poultice ; or the raw vegetable matter may be chopped finely and mixed with lard – as described later – to make an ointment.

For the tonic, one must chop the required plant very finely and bring slowly to the boil in about half a pint of water in a closed saucepan ; the amount of foliage is difficult to determine without a practical demonstration, but since the resultant liquid is a tonic and not a refined drug, it is impossible to harm the ailing animal by giving it too strong a concentration – some of the nutrients will inevitably be destroyed in the process, and the strength of the brew will also depend on the species of herb used as well as its condition.

Once the water has boiled for two or three minutes allow it to stand overnight in a non-metallic container and strain it in the morning to produce the liquid tonic.

The preparation must be stored in an airtight, non-metallic container out of direct sunlight, but even with these precautions it has a shelf life of no more than a week.

A poultice is made from much larger pieces of foliage dropped into water already on the boil, and allowed to cool for two or three hours ; it is then ready for use by simple application to the infected or injured area on the animal's body. If the plant is one whose leaves are not big enough to handle, the chopped fragments can be packed into an empty tea bag before steeping ; indeed, for poultices that are intended to go on the animal's eye, this is the only acceptable method of application.

Between treatments – no animal will tolerate a wet leaf on its fur for very long, unless it is very ill (when a vet should already have been consulted) – the poultice can be returned to the water, but at the end of the day the preparation must be discarded : it has no shelf life at all.

Ointments for external use are a little more complex. The plant, chopped as finely as possible, is stirred into a quarter pound of pure

INTERNAL MEDICINE DOSAGE CHART

Animal	Dose under 13 weeks	Adult	Mother with young
Hamster/ Gerbil	$\frac{1}{4}$—$\frac{1}{2}$ tsp. daily	1 tsp. daily	1—1$\frac{1}{2}$ tsp. daily
Rats	$\frac{1}{2}$—1 tsp. daily	2 tsp. daily	2—3 tsp. daily
Mice	Up to $\frac{1}{4}$ tsp. daily	$\frac{1}{2}$—1 tsp. daily	1 tsp. daily
Rodents under 3 in.	As mice	As mice	As mice
Rodents under 9 in.	As rats	As rats	As rats

Internal medicines are best given in the animal's drinking water. If the animal refuses to drink the water, the taste can be disguised by adding the medicine to cow's milk, or, alternatively, the drinking water and medicine can be sweetened slightly with honey.

cooking lard that has been melted in a saucepan. The mixture is simmered for at least twenty minutes, with the saucepan lid in place to avoid undue evaporation as well as to reduce the risk of fire from the molten fat. Let the preparation cool a little before pouring it into jars where it can be allowed to set. This type of ointment can be kept for many months, but must never be used to treat injury or infection near an animal's eyes.

Knowing how to prepare the plants, we are now able to consider which to prepare and for which purpose :

Coltsfoot leaves and stem are particularly useful as the raw material for poultices on abscesses ; as a tonic they can help in the recovery from colds and chills.

Clover – any part of the plant – makes a particularly good tonic for a successful breeding programme.

Chickweed is rich in minerals and its leaves and stem make a good tonic for general upsets, while a chickweed ointment is beneficial on skin or fur ailments. The tonic can also be applied on cotton-wool dabs to clean up sore eyes.

Shepherd's Purse has already had its astringent properties praised as a straightforward food, but a tonic made from the plant is also useful in cleaning cuts and grazes, while an ointment form will help in healing.

Plantain leaves also contain a strong healing agent and can be made into a poultice or an ointment for external use on any form of wound, particularly bites and sores ; eye infections and injuries may be treated with the poultice version only.

Dandelion leaves and flowers make a good medicine for blood conditioning as well as a general pick-me-up ; strong doses make a good laxative – for humans, too, as noted by the colloquial French name of the plant, *pissenlit* ('wet the bed').

Groundsel contains an antiseptic agent and is rich in minerals, particularly iron, thus making the plant ideal for a general tonic. Poultice or ointment made from the plant can be used on skin infections.

Recommended doses for adult animals are one teaspoonful per day, with half this amount for young stock ; a mother with young may have one and a half teaspoonfuls daily.

Treatment of Common Ailments

Abscess
Caused either by infected bites from other animals or from scratches from other sources, an abscess first shows itself as a slight swelling around the infected area, enlarging with time.

The treatment involves bathing with warm water containing a mild antiseptic – the plantain lotion if not a proprietary brand – and when the abscess breaks, gently squeezing it until all the poison is drained out. A vet should be consulted if the infection is large or in an awkward area.

Colds and Chills
Caused by damp or draught, with the obvious symptoms of sneezing and shivering, plus loss of appetite, colds cannot be cured in rodents any more than in man. However, the animal should be removed to a hospital box or similar cage, with the sides slightly smeared with a vapour inhalant such as Vick and the temperature maintained between 18 ° C. and 21 °C. Cod-liver oil may be added to the food. Since pneumonia has the selfsame symptoms the vet must be consulted if recovery is at all slow.

Diarrhoea
With obvious diagnosis, this is cured by removing all green food and moist mixtures from the diet, restricting it to a totally dry menu until the symptoms clear.

Minor Cuts and Bites
The result of play, battle, or accidental fall, these minor abrasions may be treated with warm water with a dilution of antiseptic – including those from the herbal cures. Major cuts must be treated by a veterinary surgeon.

These maladies sum up those which can effectively be helped with first aid, but they do not sum up the illnesses which can afflict one's pets. Some are the result of dietary deficiency and can be remedied by altering the feeding pattern, while others call for immediate recourse to a veterinary surgeon.

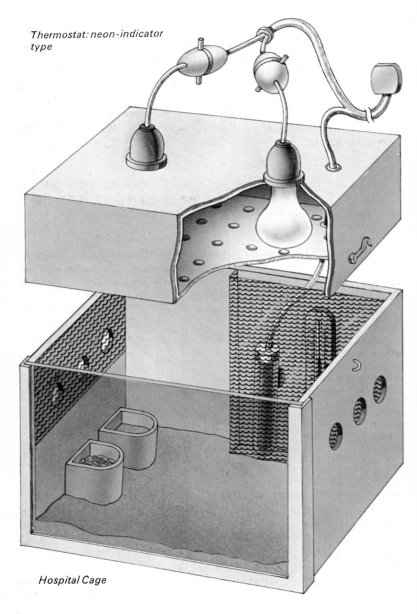

Thermostat: neon-indicator type

Hospital Cage

40

'Freezing'

Occasionally a gerbil, on being handled, will freeze, with its forefeet outstretched and with the only sign of life being a slight tremble. This is a transient thing, the cause of which is not known, but on the assumption that the theory of Vitamin B deficiency is correct, the animal should have its diet fortified with extra bran or a crushed brewers' yeast tablet. On the other assumption, that the rigidity is caused by excessive heat from the hand — however strange, in a creature of the hot deserts — the gerbil should be returned to its cage and left to recover.

Nasal Sores

Apart from bathing with mild antiseptic, there is no real treatment for this; it is caused by activity in burrowing and gnawing. Avoid using wood chippings on the floor, and use peat as a substitute.

Greasy Fur

In the wild state, the gerbil exudes natural oil onto its fur to check water evaporation, the oil evaporates instead. If its living conditions in captivity are too humid, then the oil, which is still being exuded, will not be able to evaporate and will result in greasy fur. There is no cure — certainly the fur must not be washed. The prevention of its recurrence involves moving the cage to a more amenable position. The animal will eventually groom itself clean by rolling in the floor-covering material.

Eye Injuries

These are serious in either animal. After an initial antiseptic bathe the pet must be taken to a veterinary surgeon.

Wet Tail

This illness usually spells a death sentence on the hamster which catches it. Very contagious, it is evident by loss of appetite and condition, and particularly by the wet fur around the anus — but it must not be confused with diarrhoea.

The cause is not known, but the disease is believed to be a form of dysentery or internal cancer, probably resulting from bad management, dirty cages, or dirty food. The vet must be consulted at once; he may be able to save the animal with the use of antibiotics if caught early, otherwise death will almost certainly result. Since the disease is extremely contagious the cage of the affected animal must be thoroughly disinfected, preferably with a blow lamp, and all its bedding must be burned. Everything with which the animal has come into contact must be similarly disinfected, and the breeder must not touch any other animal or its cage without thoroughly washing his hands.

Sleepiness
A sleepy hamster, very reluctant to wake, may be in partial hibernation. If this is suspected, due to the season and the temperature, the animal may be allowed to complete the process, with extra bedding provided, or it may be induced to stay awake for the winter, An animal, once completely hibernated, must be allowed to complete its sleep according to its own biological clock.

If the owner wishes to revive his pet, he must hold it in his cupped, warm hands until it revives, and thereafter keep it in a warmed position.

If, on the other hand, the season and temperature do not indicate hibernation, one may assume that the hamster – it is not a complaint of the *gerbillinae* – has an hereditary tendency to sleep, for which there is no cure at all. Such animals must not, of course, be allowed to breed.

Pouch Abscess
This is a specialized form of abscess that again attacks only the hamster, and unfortunately it too is usually fatal. Caused by food puncturing the pouch lining, and manifested by the animal's reluctance to store food in its mouth – it carries the meal, bit by bit, to its hiding place – the abscess soon results in a swollen face and bolting eyes. A veterinarian must be consulted, and he will usually advise painless destruction.

Uneven Teeth
Since rodents' teeth never stop growing, they require special attention. A broken tooth, caused by a fall or by gnawing on wire, and accentuated by a calcium or vitamin deficiency, can result in the opposing tooth growing overlong.

The treatment should be composite: the animal should have more calcium and Vitamin D, should have a piece of tree branch to gnaw, and must have its teeth levelled off by a veterinarian.

Shock
Usually resulting from a fall, shock immobilizes the animal, which must be made warm but otherwise left to recover unaided – fussing

can do more harm than good. When the animal recovers it should have a drink of warm, sweetened milk, but if recovery is slow it becomes a case for the veterinarian.

Bald Patches
There are three causes: rubbing on playthings, such as the central spindle of a treadmill; subcutaneous parasites; or Vitamin C deficiency.

The first cause is evident if the sore is on the spine. The suspicion of parasites should call for the cage to be cleaned out and the animal dusted with a flea powder recommended for cats – *not* for dogs. Parasites can usually be confirmed if the animal spends more time than usual in its grooming. The vitamin deficiency is remedied by adding greenstuff to the diet, remembering that excess will cause diarrhoea.

Vitamin Deficiency
This covers an entire gamut of minor upsets, each the result of a specific deficiency. It should never occur in the well-managed stud, but any animal which has a dull coat, is slow in its movements, shows a poor appetite, and has sunken eyes, should be suspected. The breeder must examine the animal's diet for a possible deficiency.

Motherhood Difficulties
There are two difficulties which may occur: incapacity to lactate sufficiently and excess nervousness.

The first has already been covered in the chapter on breeding – the mother may be too young or the litter too large. Apart from adding powdered milk to the diet the only remedy is to foster some or all of the litter.

Nervousness in the nursing mother is frequently caused by a too-inquisitive owner. He must leave the female in peace and soothe her nerves by increasing her intake of Vitamin B.

The breeder will seldom experience any ailment that does not fit somewhere in this list, the exception being wet patches on the side of the body of an adult hamster. This is not an illness at all, but is merely an indication that the scent glands are functioning and the animal is in its sexual prime.

Exhibiting

How good are your gerbils? Are your hamsters in the best possible condition? These questions, and many more, will sooner or later cry out to be answered; and the only way to find out is to go to a show as an exhibitor.

With hamsters and gerbils enjoying the popularity that they do, it should not prove very difficult to find a small town show, or even a larger agricultural-society exhibition, where the animals can be put to the ultimate test.

When the time comes, the two most important factors to remember are the two Ps – preparation and presentation. Assuming the animals are in perfect health and fully tamed – and those which are enetered for standard sections comply as near as possible – the two Ps are more important than everything else together.

Preparation begins several days before the actual show with a modification of the animals' diet so they do not sully their appearance. Carrot should be omitted to avoid its juices discolouring the fur, and cabbage should also be omitted not later than two days before, to eliminate the rank smell of urine on the actual day.

Stains on the fur can be removed by dampening the area very slightly and gently rubbing in cornflour. When it is dry, it should be brushed out, equally gently, with a cat-grooming brush, the process being repeated if necessary. The animal can then be placed in a grooming box, described later, to allow it to finish the process naturally.

This method of stain removal, although by far the best way, calls for two points to be stressed: the danger of really wetting the fur, which can lead to chills or worse; and the moral aspect of the process. A number of clubs consider this to be unfair practice, but since the great majority of breeders do it, unfair or not, it has become a fact of the showbench life. The Gerbil Society rules state that the practice may be adopted provided no traces of the cornflour or chalk are found at the time of exhibiting.

The grooming box is an invaluable little tool in the process of preparation. Anything from a well-ventilated biscuit tin to a specially built cage, 12in x 6in x 6in, the grooming box is essentially a container well filled with fresh hay and whitewood sawdust, in which the animal is allowed to burrow, and so groom itself, for at least an hour. While this grooming is useful at any time – the animals enjoy the diversion – it is particularly useful in the days before the show, and also at the show itself, before the animal goes

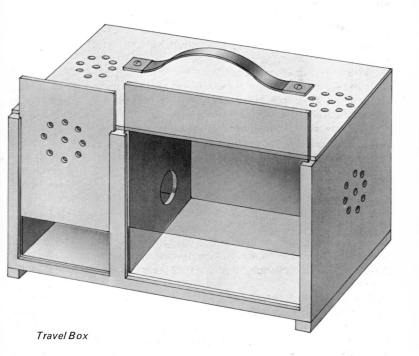

Travel Box

45

into its exhibition cage.

However, troubles lie in store on the journey from the stud to the show, particularly if unescorted rail travel is entailed. The cleaned and groomed animal must have food for the trip, but it cannot have water since the risk of spillage is far too great, even from a gravity jar. The food should be totally dry, and the moisture made available in the form of a slice of raw potato.

The final task in the preparation of the animal is its last brush-up. As it comes out of the grooming cage its fur should be rubbed gently with a pure silk cloth, in stroking motions from head to tail, until the coat takes on a really lustrous sheen.

Presentation is concerned mainly with the show cage itself and its contents, other than the animal.

While food and water are usually allowed during judging and exhibiting of gerbils it is still advisable not to include a drink as a slight spillage can ruin all the work done up to this moment. The gerbil-cage interior should be as clean as possible, with food reduced to a bare token and with a minimum of bedding – hamsters will be disqualified if the cage contains a trace of either bedding or food, and also if the sawdust on the floor is not white. These requirements are laid down not only to make the process of judging easier (no judge wants to dig into excess bedding to find the competitor's animal) and to avoid distracting detail, but also to impose a code of uniformity so that there is no possibility of an adjudicator being accused of favouritism: he must judge each animal on its merit without having the least idea of its owner's identity. The only identification allowed on any cage is the official pen label, stuck on the top left corner, and written in a code which the show marshal alone can understand.

It is therefore obvious that uniformity in the cage itself is also necessary, unless the animal being shown is in the 'pet' class where some degree of tolerance is allowed.

The appropriate societies have exact specifications of the cages for both hamsters and gerbils, as well as lists of approved manu-facturers, but as a guide the hamster cage is 6in high on a base 8in x 6in. The gerbil exhibition cage – known as the Touchwood pen, after my own stud prefix – stands 6in high on a base $8\frac{1}{4}$in x 6in, with a large slice of its volume cut away by a sloping grille front.

The catch on this sloping door must be foolproof – without extending this compliment to the judge himself! Since the animal needs to be taken from its cage and examined in detail – including

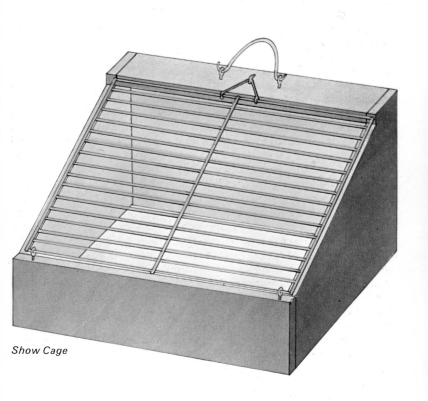

Show Cage

an assessment of its tameness — the catch must be effective without involving wasting time in untangling a foot or more of wire.

If, after all the preparations, the animal was unplaced, there is no need for despondency. After the show, approach the judge and ask him exactly why he faulted a certain animal and how the defects can be made good the next time. Judges, after all, have risen from the ranks of the exhibitors and are usually keen to impart any information which will result in the advancement of the hobby: a disgruntled exhibitor is one who can so very easily quit the show benches for ever, leaving the judge in an unenviable position.

Winner or loser, the exhibitor should now begin a simple card index of his results, giving show details, code index of animals shown, results, and comments.

But for the victor, the spoils. While the cash value of the prize — a simple card or a rosette — is nil, the reward has come not so much in the prize itself, which is the end result, but in the winning of it, which can be the culmination of days, weeks, or even months of hard but very interesting and rewarding work.

Show standards

Hamsters

Since the first Golden Hamster was introduced to the public, breeders all over the world have been striving with great success to produce colour mutations, but the ultimate aim of a black hamster has still not been achieved. However, these are some of the variations that are to be found from almost any breeder:

Cream Hamsters

Red Eyed Cream; Ruby Eyed Cream. Although these two standards are so very similar, they are nonetheless distinct. The Ruby has a much darker colour in its eyes, and also tends to show a fleshy colouration on the rich milky-cream fur which it shares with the Red.

Black Eyed Cream. This differs not only in its obvious eye colouration, but also in the deeper, richer coat colour, which verges on black on the ears.

Golden Hamsters

These are subdivided according to shading, but all have black eyes:

Normal Golden has a golden-brown top coat lightly ticked with black but showing greyish roots to the hairs. The belly is almost white while the ears are dark grey.

Dark Golden hamsters have, despite their name, a deep-red sheen to their coat with the black ticking very much more prominent: the ears are black.

Light Golden aptly describes the coat which is almost devoid of black ticking. The belly is white.

Grey Hamsters

Dominant Grey. At first appearing as a medium-dark grey, the coat on closer examination reveals an almost dark grey, overlaid with a flesh-coloured tint. The overall effect of this coat is pleasing, and it is offset by the black eyes and the almost black ears.

Dark Grey. This is darker than the Dominant Grey and lacks the fleshy tint, but its eyes and ears are the same.

Light Grey. A silvery tint to the grey fur, and distinctive red eyes, easily make this variation recognizable.

Marked Colours

There are many variations of marked colours which in most

Red-eyed Cream Hamster

Normal Golden Hamster

Banded Hamster

instances are merely crosses from other colours : the three listed are the best known, and the variations within each one are myriad.

Banded. An animal of almost any colour can have a mid section of its fur perfectly white, much like a saddleback in reverse. Another way of describing it would be to imagine a bandage completely encircling the animal's girth. While many such mutations tend to have the band broken or with uneven edges, the ideal is a uniform area with clean edges. The variations are innumerable, e.g. Golden Cinnamon Banded ; Light Grey Banded.

Piebald. As in the horse, the piebald hamster is basically white with patches of other colour – *not* skewbald, in which white is the intrusive colour. In the perfect specimen the patches should be evenly matched and with distinct edges.

Tortoiseshell and White. The cat-owner will easily recognize this description : an animal with a coat of any one colour which is overlaid with white and gold patches. The ideal specimen must have clear identification and uniformity.

White Hamsters
Albino, sometimes known as *Pink Eyed White,* is the pure pigmentless form : totally white fur with pink eyes.

Dark Eared Albino. An odd variation of the albino is the one which develops a dark tint on the ears shortly after birth, turning almost black with maturity.

Black Eyed White. Another variation of the albino, with black pigmentation in the eyes – some may also have dark patches inside the ears.

Some other colours
Cinnamon, but in fact slightly more orangey, and with the colour uniform throughout the upper body, paling to almost white on the belly ; the eyes are red and the ears have a brownish tinge.

Honey. It may also have a few dark guard hairs, but ideally should be without them. The honey colour extends to the belly as well, though paler, with the ears grey and the eyes red.

Rust. Very similar to Cinnamon except that the fur has darker guard hair – ticking – all over. The eyes, though black, are not dominant, and the ears are a medium brown.

Satin Coated hamsters can be of any colour but must have the beautiful shot-silk effect of the satin-like fur.

Sepia hamsters have frequently been confused with Dominant Grey ones, but the Sepia animal has a beige colour rather than grey

Albino Hamster

and lacks the fleshy tinge. The standard also calls for a uniform dark ticking, which in poor specimens tends to spoil the appearance altogether. The eyes are black and the ears dark grey.

Yellow. This description covers a wide range of shades from rich apricot to pale cream.

There have been several additions recently to the standards, of which these are noteworthy :

Smoke Pearl. The entire coat is of light pearl-grey, evenly shaded right down to the skin and with no tendency to turn tawny. The eyes are black, the ears dark grey.

Blond. With red eyes, this hamster is blond everywhere else.

Long Haired. The colour and markings must conform to that of any one recognized variety, but the animal is in a class by itself because of its fur, which must be as long as possible and fine and dense.

Rex. As in Long Haired, except that the coat must be 'rex', curly.

Dove. The entire coat is a medium dove-grey, with a darker base ; the belly is white. There are clearly defined cheek flashes which must not be prominent. Eyes black ; ears dove-grey.

The hamster show standards, as designated by the British Federation of Hamster Clubs, gives an animal 100 points at the start of the exhibition, and penalizes it for any variation from the accepted norm. Diseased or intractable animals, those with food or bedding, as well as those in cages open to suspicion of carrying identification, will be disqualified. Excess fat, bones, or fright (other than that caused during the show) carry a further penalty of up to 5 points each.

Points are allocated thus :

Colour and markings	30
Type	15
Fur	15
Size	15
Condition	15
Eyes	5
Ears	5

Elaboration of the system of marking :

Colour — *as specified for the variety on preceding pages.*

Type — *The body shall be broad, the head large and well set, and the nose blunt.*

Long-hair Hamster

Rex Hamster

Fur – *short, but dense and soft all over.*
Size – *The animal shall be large but not fat.*
Condition – *alert and fit, with a healthy coat.*
Eyes – *as large as possible without protruding, and set well apart.*
Ears – *large and erect.*

Gerbils

The National Mongolian Gerbil Society has also laid down standards for animals exhibited in shows under its control. Points of main concern are that the animal must be alert at all times, but easily handled. Its fur which should have a healthy sheen and not be moulting, must be as thick and as short as possible, and soft to the touch, with the belly fur really dense.

The gerbil must be large without being fat – allowance being made for the fact that females are smaller – and its tail must be at least as long as the body in the adult specimen; since immature animals have relatively shorter tails, this, too, is considered in judging. The head must be short and broad, set well into the body with large, bright eyes widely set without bulging. The ears must be fairly small, carried erect, and must not be too rounded.

There is a detailed code to be followed in relation to the animal's colours: those of the back and flanks must be a soft golden-red – the colour of the desert – evenly covered with black ticking over the back and sides, and underlaid with dark-grey fur at skin level; the belly must be as white as possible. The tail's upper surface must match that of the back, while the underside must be slightly paler; it must be ticked with black and show a distinct ridge the full length, ending in a dark, almost black, tuft.

The ears, free from ticking, must be light grey, bordered with a soft golden-red. The black eyes must have a distinct circle of light-grey hair around them; the claws must also be black.

Variations are fewer than in the hamsters, being restricted virtually to the Albino Standard, the White Spots, and the range of colours described as Dilute.

Dilute varies from the basic standard in these points: the fur on the back and sides must be light gold with no ticking; it must be pale to light grey at skin level. The same shade should also edge the ears. This standard does not call for a ridge down the centre of the tail.

Normal Golden Gerbil

*Dilute Canadian White Spot
Gerbil*

The **Canadian White Spot** may be of normal or dilute colour, but showing two white marks, as large as possible, one on the forehead and the other on the base of the neck; the nose should have a fine furry covering and the claws must be neutrally coloured; variations will be penalized.

The **White Spot** is as above, except that the single spot must be on the forehead.

Two other varieties: the **Dark Tailed White** complies with the Albino standard up to the age of 13 weeks, thereafter having a dark ridge along the crest of the tail. The **Grey Bellied** is a mutation on any normal or dilute colour, having, as the name implies, a grey underside.

The animal entering the exhibition carries a total of 100 points, allocated thus:

Colour	20
Condition	20
Type	15
Fur	15
Size	15
Eyes	5
Tuft on tail	5
Ears	5

from which deductions are made as the entrant varies from the accepted class norm. It may also lose up to 20 points for sores or nervousness; up to 10 on obesity, moulting, or stained fur, and 5 points for a dirty show pen. Disease or intractability will result in disqualification.

Index